# AGAIN

# AGAIN

poems

## Lynne Knight

SIXTEEN RIVERS PRESS

Copyright © 2009 by Lynne Knight
All rights reserved

Printed in Canada

Published by Sixteen Rivers Press
P.O. Box 640663
San Francisco, CA 94164-0063
www.sixteenrivers.org

Cover and interior design: David Bullen
Cover photograph: Jorden Blucher

ISBN: 978-0-9767642-8-1
Library of Congress Control Number: 2008935616

*for Michael*

# CONTENTS

Prologue — 13

## One

Early Measures — 17
Wanting — 19
O, Penelope! — 21
A Sentimental Education — 23
Dust — 24
Cup — 25
Love in the Late Afternoon — 26
The Language of Love — 27
Against Order — 29
For All It's Worth — 31
In a Time of Strife — 32
The Door — 33
Untimely Snow — 34

## Two

The Mood of Longing — 39
Bulimia — 40
Beyond the Painting — 42
Ghost Sailing — 44
The Severing — 46
The Story Behind Her Insomnia — 48
Rifts — 51
After What Was — 52

| | |
|---|---|
| Driving Through the Valley | 53 |
| Resuming Quiet | 54 |
| As If Love Were a Room | 56 |

## *Three*

| | |
|---|---|
| The Obsessive Gaze | 59 |

## *Four*

| | |
|---|---|
| De Kooning's Woman | 71 |
| Elegy, with Towpath and Mule | 72 |
| In a Time of Mourning | 74 |
| The Deepest Blue | 75 |
| Prayer for the Dying | 77 |
| The Cloud | 79 |
| The Gold Basket | 80 |
| Recovery | 81 |
| Continuous Meadow | 84 |
| Then | 85 |
| Reprise | 86 |
| | |
| Acknowledgments | 89 |
| About the Author | 91 |

# AGAIN

# Prologue

While we slept, such heavy rain swept past
it shook the last roses loose. They lay
smashed on the deck this morning, their petals
scattered like big white tears. I shouldn't say
a thing so sentimental. But there they were.
And you, my father, so long dead, why
should I not expect you to be everywhere,
reminding me how little will be left—
vague ache in my own daughter's heart
as she sweeps the steps after rain whose mercy
is all in the coming, the coming again.

# ONE

# Early Measures

Her sister sang the song of the beast,
all breathy and pull-up-the-covers,
and then she slept, little puffs of dream
from across the room, while the beast lay
in the dust under her own bed, hissed
he would get her, ankle by ankle grab hold
then pull her down to eat her, skin and bone.

There was no safe hiding place. Her mother
warned never to hold the pillow over her face
or she'd turn blue. Blue like the baby
her mother had not brought home the afternoon
her sister had sworn, *It's inside her suitcase.*
The suitcase kept still while her mother
held them too hard, then went to her room.

Her sister went to the suitcase, opened it.
Silkiness, bunched up like a wrong answer.
That night her sister whispered the beast
would follow them everywhere, even if
they moved to Arabia and wore veils
and perfumes, the beast would be able
to tell who they were. He had eaten

their brother, had a taste for their blood.
The only thing that would save them was song.
*It's a really really long song*, her sister said.
*But it's the only thing. It starts out, "Star light."*
She leaned at the dark and sang again: *"Star light."*
She leaned more, listening. *You just have to
make it up as you go. If he likes it, you're free.*

# Wanting

*Knightgown,* they called me, and how I wished
a nightgown would descend on me whenever
I stood before them, to hide my fat girl body
from their mocking eyes and tongues.
*You may be the smartest girl in the class,*
*but you're also the fattest!* All these years later,
I can still name the one who shouted that,
remember looking down at the rough dirt

playground, strewn with maple seeds,
then back up to the old brick building where,
the day before, I'd been made to go recite
the Gettysburg Address, lean speech
the fat fourth-grade phenomenon reeled off
to every class, blood rising high in
high school boys' faces as they laughed
behind their hands. *Now we are engaged . . .*

I grew to hate my arms and legs, the way
my stomach sat like something extra
in my lap. My whole body seemed extra,
an outer fleshy suit sealed tight to the one
I knew was truly mine, the long slim lithe one
like my sister's, like those of girls in books I read,
or almost all the other girls who lived, but when
I climbed trees to dream of it, the branches

threatened to give way, and I trembled,
clutching the firm, fat trunk, my twin.
Being slow at books would be far worse,
but how much worse I seemed to know
less and less. Then, thirteen, I fasted
during Lent. My clothes began to drift past
the extra body I was killing off, uneaten
sweet by sweet. I loved denying her. I loved

the strange sensation of walking light
into a room. Most of all, I loved the end
of taunts. Then one night in the mirror I saw
the fat one pouring back inside the shadows
of my thinness. She looked so lost.
Still, I turned away. But she never left me.
Not even the cries of lovers alter her. Night
after night, she lies in my arms, wanting.

# O, Penelope!

The nuns of Mount St. Mary's loved Penelope, whose skills
they urged us all to emulate: She fought off men. She used
her mind. Long after we'd read the prose version, slightly
sexed down (those nights with Calypso eclipsed),

Penelope was steadily invoked—wily, though not quite
as wily as Mr. Wiliness himself; patient, so that even Job
might take his text from her; discreet in her appetites,
which the nuns chose to ignore, never quizzing us on

the scar (since God forbid we should mention
the man's thigh) or the bed with its highly unusual post.
No, ours was the Penelope of Attic vases,
gowned, accepting gifts from suitors, or sitting

at her loom, elbow on knee, head on hand, thoughtful
Telemachus beside her as she figured out her next move
now that the maids had betrayed her. No more unravelling!
But she was shining among all women, the gods would intervene ...

Heretical, yes, but we mustn't blame the Greeks;
at least [*finger wag*] they believed in something.
And they liked a good story: Odysseus stringing the bow,
stripping off his rags to guide the fatal arrows

to the suitors until the great hall smoked with blood ...
Not that we were being asked to condone violence.
But anything to preserve virtue! [*sigh*] Anything!
No wonder so many of us headed straight

for the back seat of a car. Why wait any longer?
We wanted to test our pluck and ingenuity...
and then, hand sliding down a bare thigh,
whisper, *Oh, I'd know you anywhere* . . .

# A Sentimental Education

Then I thought all I had to do was close my eyes
and let him take me, slow and soft
before the rush of clothes and parts and wet.

Then I thought I could say what they said in books
(*oh this, oh yes*).

Then I thought my body was enough
even with its inadequate breasts and secrets.

Then I thought any lover who wanted me had some claim
as if I were land or a building.

Then the dreams said *Oh Lord what is this child*.

Then I did not wrestle with conscience or scripture.
I did what I did.

Then I thought forgiveness would come like rain or wind.

Then I waited.

# Dust

A carriage rumbles in the distant past
you read about in novels where young girls dream of love
as something that will save them,
not knowing how the store of grief
accumulates like grain spilled on a wooden floor

Whatever is not eaten by small foragers
turns to dust then less than dust and all this time
the women go on apprehending the vacuity
inside their girlhood dreams

They manage all their disappointments with a grace
not recognized by any of the religions
requiring submission

Some nights, sleepless, they walk from room to room,
their long robes dusting random surfaces, like women in a novel
wanting to escape the fate that's written
into every breath before it's taken

# Cup

In one dream, I fled the armies of the night.
They meant me harm, even destruction,
and I fled across rivers, mountains; the continents
passed beneath me as if I were a bird.

*You have an illness*, they said. *Many suffer
from similar things. Swallow this.*

You can imagine how long it took,
swallowing the armies, the rivers, the paths
of migrating birds. But eventually
I was there with nothing in the background.
A blankness such as arrives when you wake too suddenly
and forget where you are, even who.

I ate the amnesia like snow
I had eaten as a child, shoving it in
with both hands so numb with cold I barely apprehended
they were part of what I could call mine.

It is hard to tell stories without time
and furniture. But think of the instant you lift
your foot to place it on the next step.
Whole histories can occur in interstices.

Then they are forgotten. This is no cause for mourning
or regret. The thing is the day
with its hours and cries. The cup in your hands,
solid as any prayer you need to say.

# Love in the Late Afternoon

There's hardly a moment too sweet
for its own good. At first you want to leave
without touching anything at all,
but the scene is always far more ambiguous.
Who knows how long it plays?
There are crisp sequences, the sound of wings
escaping all the time limits—
the concentration of the intricate.
Nothing sinister, nothing too stout-hearted.
A little star-crossed clumsiness,
but no hint of the doomed or humorless.

Then the stars, as in an earthly paradise.
Not really what you had in mind as aftermath,
but given all your need to count
what you have coming, you don't complain.
If you didn't have a body, the hollow
that you feel now would be deeper. All the vowels
inside your name would drain away.

# The Language of Love

      after John Singer Sargent's *Fumée d'ambre gris*


What country is this? The woman stands
above a censer, smoke of ambergris
floating up under her wide pagoda hat.
Everything except her mouth and skin,

the ornate rug she stands on,
and her loose sleeves' deep red rims
glows white, threatened by the censer's
smoke. But wait—the pagoda hat is more

a veil, close up, coarsely woven—
she's not Japanese but Moroccan,
with an elaborate silver cross
hung round her neck. An exotic,

letting the heavy scent of ambergris
slow her blood until the day's a dream
the way the painting of it is, and neither
part of time the way we measure it.

I want to say it's like the time
we take when we make love,
letting the body go where it will,
slow then quick then slow again

like smoke climbing the stone portico
whose shade the woman stands in.
But it's more like wanting to make love—
watching you across the room

in late-afternoon shadows, thinking
I can take in the scent of your warm skin
again, again, I can come to you
as anyone, depending on my tongue.

# Against Order

*Tear the line into pieces.*
                                      *Open it out:*
    *Let silence be*
                    *part of all that must be*
                                  *said.*

I can't.                      I can't.
It looks so disorganized. I want
to move it like furniture
back into place.

*It's a curse, your obsession for order,*
my lover says, wanting me
                    wild—

So, to justify myself, I point out
that light in the night sky
may be traveling, but the stars stay
where they are.

Or do they?
What if some night Cassiopeia
fell apart,
splashed down like water?

What use the well-appointed bed,
the vacuumed rug,
the alphabetically arranged books
if a star came splashing down
like water, fiery water,
burning everything in its path?

All my molecules about to scatter—

just the thought of it makes me clutch
the sheets, press myself into the mattress—

but ah, the wonder of it, to be
moving inside my lover's
arms then, any second bound

        to explode—

# For All It's Worth

Life rearranged itself in the dream
so that he could be mine. Letters from Utah
played a role, and when I finally saw him—
my skirt lashed away by wind so that I held
a big piece of grade-school paper to hide

the cellulite on my thighs—I saw he had grown
his hair long and dyed it black. His pomade
stiffened the loose strands into licorice.
His nose was so huge I wondered how
we would kiss. Then he said something

about politics. I remembered we had been
on opposing sides, and I saw I would never
be able to make love to someone who believed
what he believed. I felt desire drain from me
in the dream, just as I realized he was already

dead. I woke thinking, *Why Utah?*
*Because any sorrow is a great salt lake?*
But now I feel double shame. First,
for wanting him, then for changing him into
a cartoon so I could stop wanting him.

If any of this sounds familiar, maybe
you, too, could bear reminder that the heart
is a small organ, vulnerable, subject,
beautiful in the abstract but ugly up close,
beating for all its worth, either way.

# In a Time of Strife

We crouched to see marsh violets while the sky
swept past us, clouds of no known shape
while it was night. Explorer's gentian shook
around our ankles and we knew their blue would be

the blue of sky if it were day, so when the moon
began to climb so rapidly we almost couldn't follow,
we turned as if to say, *What mountain have we climbed?*
but then the alpine aster broke apart like stars

exploding toward some grand, apocalyptic ending
just as we heard Scotch bluebells shift and bend,
a pealing sound against the wind—we called it wind
but it felt more like the back of night—and so descent

became the only thought we clung to: a rope we held
tight, running, stumbling, until our palms rubbed
almost raw, though there are never signs of prayer
once prayer is done and sky resumes its cover.

# The Door

> after *Taos Doors*, a photograph by Heather Holston

The doors were out back, leaned against acacias,
flatbed wagons, hay rakes. Old doors, that had opened
and closed thousands of times, though now
the houses were gone, the buildings, there was nothing

to open into, to close upon. She walked slowly, seeing
her old lovers—blue door, weatherbeaten door,
door with the beautiful flaw in the middle. Her body
like a door to them, opening, opening, then

staying shut. Not out of malice or even lack
of desire. Just time. Time at work until the doors
sound like wind, opening, shutting, waiting
for release into a new gesture, someone rushing,

calling out *Hold the door, please!*—exactly what
she tells the proprietor now, of the teak door
time has stained the color of the sea near
the door of the horizon, receding from reach.

## Untimely Snow

I walk into the woods where snow
  falls so quietly I feel myself enclosed
inside a snow-filled globe, souvenir
  containing oaks already frozen and deer

feeding on red berries I can't name
  because I have forgotten everything
in this untimely snow that falls over me,
  the oaks, and deer; even if I shout loud

to see if the deer will stir, I won't know
  if it's the world I'm lost in or the scene
made in miniature to resemble the world
  so that someone longing for the time

when walking through snowy woods
  meant walking through snowy woods—
not an attempt to numb the heart's pain
  or escape the small betrayals of the day—

someone longing for that time can take
  the souvenir in hand and say, *Look,*
*this is just like the woods I used to walk in*
  *when I was a kid,* then stare past the listener

remembering other woods, other snow,
  other pain and betrayal following
while the actual snow goes on falling
  so fast now that even the names

on the stones in the old graveyard
>   beyond the red berries the deer still
feed on—how one thing slips into another—
>   even the names disappear under snow.

# TWO

# The Mood of Longing

The condition contrary to fact
where the verb turns weirdly plural
as if a ghost had grabbed your hand

—*If I were you*—

to show you the difference
between what was or was not
in a realm you never entered
since it was contrary to fact

—*If I were you*—

though imaginable, the way ghosts
could be imagined entering the bodies
of the dead, wearing their favorite clothes,
whispering comfort

—*If I were you*—

even if their bodies turned to air
as grievers reached for
one last touch

—*If I were you*—

You would never have left me

# Bulimia

        Gr. *boulimia* < *buos*, ox + *limos*, hunger

I slipped into bed beside him with my clove-sweet mouth
that had known the hunger of an ox an hour earlier
when I'd crept down to the kitchen to stand in the dark,
eating from cartons and boxes.

Some nights he would wake, want me.
I would lie still and run, he had no idea how far.
Afterward I would hold him in my arms
the way I sometimes held one of his shirts,
thinking of the ways to measure emptiness.

It was not what you would call a life,
though it was a life. I kept hearing the word
*ungoverned*. Even the trees knew no restraint,
banging against the back of the house, the low sky.

By day I never let on. I took my body,
walked it into a schoolroom, gave instruction.
I was careful never to scrape my knuckles
or cause other signs, so I did not look
like someone with such hunger.

But I was yoked to it.
One day, reading the dictionary
while my students bent to their work, I went from *bulimia*
to *ox*, stared down at the words *draft animal*.
I felt myself tear open. More holes to fill . . .

Long after I broke away, I could still feel
the yoke at my shoulders,
the dark shape dragging behind me.

# Beyond the Painting

*after Winslow Homer's* Farmyard Scene

What a din, all these turkeys and chickens
scratching a bit of bare earth for feed
scattered earlier by the farmer's wife,

who's behind the east window kneading
though her hands ache from arthritis
and she's about to scream with all there is

to do—not the idyll you imagined
when you first looked at the farmhouse,
the apple tree, the scud of bright clouds.

What's more, the farmer, even this early
in the day, reeks of whiskey but can't say why
he feels so desperate when there's food

for the table and a cellar full of jugs. He's
in the far field, plowing, readying for winter.
They've come to love winter, hunkering

in muteness by the fire. Death is nothing
to fear, they say. But think what it's doing
beyond the painting: tearing tiles from the roof,

breaking doors down, rotting sills and eaves.
The unpruned trees go sterile, grass climbs
the lilacs by the shed, which go on thriving

despite the general decay. Soon the lilacs will
go by, their dense perfume almost unbearable,
like nights of love you'll never have again.

# Ghost Sailing

The boat came slowly, sails reefed,
no one at the till. *Ghost sailing*,
the woman thought, watching from
a point just north along the shore.

The moon lay its broken path
over the bay. At moments
she felt she might glide forth,
walk across water. If ghosts

could sail... But she stood
where she was below the rush
of stars. She'd left her lover
sleeping, then driven down the hill,

their pointless argument resounding.
Was he planning to leave her?
The boat banged like a door
against the rocky shore. She took

a few steps toward it, thinking
someone hidden in the hull
might waken. Nothing but the mast
pressing its shadow at the water

like a sketch begun, begun again.
Then the boat listed hard, settled.
He would stir when she slipped
back into bed, reaching out

as she did now, wanting
to feel the boat's skin
but sensing it too cold
and not, anyway, hers.

## The Severing

When the dog brought the pig's head
from the farm across the street and dropped it
on the back walk, it was midsummer, warm
even deep at night, so by dawn the flies
were already stirring their hard bodies
toward it. By the time I came out to shake
crumbs from the tablecloth, the head moved
like a live thing with their gorging.

The dog lay unroused by all the buzzing,
himself gorged on brain and blood.
I didn't scream. I draped the cloth
over the porch rail and went down
to squat beside the thing. I took a stick
from the lawn, poked a little, making
flies swirl up like smoke and settle back.
The dog watched through a barely open eye.

A stupid dog, who the week before had herded
the Hannos's cows onto the farmhouse porch,
then sat and barked as they clattered back
and forth, their blank eyes spinning wild.
I poked some more and saw a pig eye
missing. The cut-off veins and gristle
clotted over bones I didn't know enough
anatomy to name. I waited there

as if for revelation. Inside the house,
the man I claimed to love had finished
with his coffee. I heard the water rinse
his cup, heard the click that lit another
cigarette. Then nothing but the flies,
moving like a heavy dream you know
you'll keep the feel of when you wake.
I touched the small red branches

of a vein high on my thigh, first sign
my legs were aging. Sometimes his tongue
moved there, moved slowly there, in ragged
circles—like the flies I brushed at then in quick
revulsion, standing as I threw the stick,
dizzying just as he came down the steps.
*What in hell*, he said, and went to get a shovel.
That afternoon a downpour washed away the stain.

I could tell you I dreamed the severed head,
sign of what I knew I had to do. But it was real,
as real as all my lies there, where I lived
another dozen years, dreaming of another
life, one that wouldn't distance me from all
I longed for. As if a life were not continuous
with longing. As if I'd ever stop those years
from meaning all they do beyond their severing.

# The Story Behind Her Insomnia

*Exposition*

If she wrote to those she had wronged,
went down on her knees,
would that be enough to atone?

*You must be doing something wrong.*
Someone come back from the dead
to rebuke her.

Even the rain won't ease.
It beats so hard she fears washout,
ruin, the house tumbling down the hillside,

the bed crashing into the coast oaks,
a tangle of blankets and limbs.
*You must be doing something wrong.*


*Rising Action*

Enter sleep potions: warm milk,
honey, herbs. Enter craving
for the slow, deep

breath beside her. *I barely
slept*, he says. *But I heard you.*
*I heard you*, she says, neither

believing the other. Doubt
takes on guises like a dream
where someone says, *I barely slept.*


*Turning Point*

Rain beating on the roof.
*You must have done something wrong.*
His voice, bundled cloth:

*I know if I slept or I didn't.*
Turning away. Turning away:
both of them, bodies

in a bed, a photograph of which says
*Rift.* Says *Look: This is not how they began.*
Neither believing the other's claims

but disguising their loss
by claiming it's a dream sleeplessness
keeps making them enter.


*Falling Action*

Someone walking across a river:
someone dead, or her feet would displace
the water: *You must be*

*doing something wrong.* She reaches
to touch him, as if the dream keeping him
so quiet might be hers.

*I'm sleeping, can't you see I'm sleeping.*
This is not how they began—tangled in
each other's limbs, the bed a ruin,

*Dénouement*

love at their lips. For solace,
they tell themselves no one escapes
loss, no one gets up from bed without it.

# Rifts

While Marten's bluebells shook and seemed to fall
then rise again in wind and rain so white
the earth seemed more like sea than earth, with all
the houses, roads, the mountain's slope just slight

declivities on the abyssal plain,
she looked beyond them to upendings, rifts
between the real and dreamed, inside the pain
she stared through like a window as cloud-drifts

arranged the sky into a fiercer sea.
Who said that nature doesn't change itself
for human moods? She was bereft. Each plea
she flung toward the abyss—that deep-sand shelf

no one can see—was met with silence rough
as his last words to her: *Enough. Enough.*

## After What Was

Caravans follow stars across deserts
that open behind your eyes when you try
to think back into time, but that direction

seems wrong, lacking the forward motion
of caravans, of time—even if the drivers
have stopped, are crouched around low fires

drinking whiskey or sweet tea, the camels
folded behind them like breathing dunes—
you could see the fleas if you concentrated,

smell the damp hairs, the windless night—
everything so unlike your own life,
with its marked roads, wall switches—

yet because you believe the heart
is the heart no matter how far you travel,
you wait for the journey to resume,

imagining they are carrying precious oils
to sell to women who have no need
to lie alone nights mourning what was.

# Driving Through the Valley

Nothing all that strange about the scene—
a field, a long-abandoned house and barn,

the wood of both gone dark with mildew
that had dulled a whitish gray with months

of California sun—but the horse beside
the barn was strange in its untethered calm,

eating dry grass with an air so resigned
it seemed familiar, someone I knew—

some woman with a hunger to be martyred
without a word, though it was hard to call

the feeding horse a martyr—yet something
close to that in spirit, meek, subdued, expecting

nothing but the next dry blade, head bent—
and then I saw the not-so-distant night—the horse

gone now, miles behind me—the night I took
the water glass he thrust at me like some rough

measure of the tears I'd wept, took it, hands
trembling, and bent my head and drank.

# Resuming Quiet

Hand on the door—gesture of escape
like that—she waits like someone in
a superstition, then shakes her head, turns
to him and says, *If everything on earth
is sacred, you'll have to spend eternities
atoning your sins*, a speech slightly ruined
in its effects by seeming rehearsed,
but he would have yawned, anyway,
affected some insouciance just to prove

this parting would not wreck his heart.
Outside—each looks, as if to authenticate
their words with time and place—
two deer move down the bank, feeding
on new acanthus. They themselves dislike
acanthus, he because his ex-wife planted it,
she because his ex-wife planted it, so
they speak with restraint, not wanting
to scare the deer off. Years before,

in this same room, they had sworn
not to make the same mistakes again,
the only oath they thought they'd need.
*I wish*, she says now, *I wish we'd taken
vows. It would gratify me, to break them
like plates. Like windows. Maybe some night
I'll come back and break all the windows,
let you wake to ruin, see how you like it.*
He waits for the melodrama to pass.

It passes. They both feel grief, yes,
and for months afterwards, but nothing
keen, nothing that much beyond
the ordinary. They see each other from
time to time—the theatre, hauling
groceries from the Bowl—and they seem
startled, then relieved, like the deer looking up
when the door finally opened,
heads dipping back as quiet resumed.

## As If Love Were a Room

That day, things began to seem a little loose
about the edges, dirt crumbling so her spade
kept slicing at the roots of penstemon and lavender
below the garden wall, words blurring till the thing
he said kept replicating like a wayward cell,

making the sky tear open, edges yielding edges,
the long night pulling the moon out of phase
till moonlight spilled like cloth inside the window
while wind blew over her as she lay curled
on the bed, trying to erase the sense of edges

cutting into her like all his quick-flung, parting words—
*I just can't be here anymore*—as if love were
a room, broken up by door and window, skylight—
exits all around while she was left there coiled
on the bed, a snake or rope, something

that could loosen at the edges, though for longer
than she could have dreamed—days, weeks,
the moon in many guises—rigidity set in and nothing
gave. Then one day she stood and stretched her body
to its edges, relieved they held her in like walls.

# THREE

# The Obsessive Gaze

> *I loved you once.*
> *It seemed so right, so neat.*
> *The moon, the month, the flower, the kiss—*
> > Eavan Boland, "Tirade for the Lyric Muse"

*Pas de deux*

When I breathe, she breathes.
When I look down, she follows.
The secrets that pass between us—

it's almost talk in code: *The house.*
*The man with the strange thumb.*
*The lost nights, the purges.*

Sometimes, though I know seven
years of bad luck might ensue,
I break her into pieces. One eye

fails, another. I vow to go on
without her, but there are so many
surfaces where I apprehend

this one I despise so obsessively,
love so obsessively, for being
the first and last who will leave me.

*Aftermathematics*

Scatter all the shards like seed.
Dim the lights.

Avoid excess of any kind.
You will still be caught wanting

your double,
your everything-the-same.

*Veiled Illusions*

No matter that her face, once
beautiful, on film was still.

Now it cracked and sagged.
Rotted.

She kept the drapes drawn. If she left the house,
she wore veiled hats.

If she had to look into the mirror,
she prepared by weeping

or drinking so much that nothing would be there
but a blur.

"*Chaplet of the Infernal Gods*"

So said Socrates, because of the narcotic
effect of narcissus, whose sweet scent
is nearly foul, like perfume masking rot.

But they sway so easily in wind.
Their small white dresses call *Come! Come!*
They long to be undone. They hold still in the sun,

suffering, pale, pliant as martyrs.
They yearn for the pool where they can be
perfectly reflected, marble flowers

that sink like the dead into earth, far
past roots, stopping only at bedrock
where they shatter into useless stars.


*Metempsychosis, with Star and Ash*

The lover's gaze is famous for its ardency—
fire in the eyes, eyes like stars.
The lover whispers, *Look
into my eyes.* And the strange exchange

of one soul with another occurs,
or is said to occur, no one knowing
exactly what the soul is, whether its substance
is transmissible, transmutable.

But certain laws of physics are immutable:
For want of fuel,
for want of oxygen,
fire dies. Can you feel the rival

myth creeping in? the blood-red bird rising
from ash? It too wants nothing more
than the adulating cry a despairing lover
longs to see mirrored: *You're back!*


*Lost Law of Thermodynamics*

At night, the stars stream fire
while other bodies, knowing they will never
travel fast enough to find
their origins, lie still and dream.

There is no room
in any bed for the quantity of dreaming
that goes on.
In this way, the universe expands.


*Fractured*

How many parts does it have, the self?
Are those it loves and fears included?
And what about its interrupted dreams—

*Reprise with Moon and Scythe*

She climbed fast, the goatlike one
behind her, bleating lust. Stones
rumbled over the earth's dry crust,
plunged into the troughs his cries

cut from air. She was too quick for
him, and disappeared. Later
he went among the shepherds,
whispering of the beautiful young girl

hiding among their herds, intent
on spells, sickness. That night
when the moon hung thin as a scythe,
they climbed to find her.

She was asleep, white limbed,
beneath a juniper. They hacked and hacked
till there was nothing but her cries,
her cries.

*Alternative Reprise*

Or she arranged to distract the wife while
the hot one dallied. She would be next,
he promised. So while he went off,

she kept the wife busy under the portico.
Should she wear her hair in three coils,
two looped over her ears then fed back

into a double loop at the base of her neck,
was she old enough for that? and
when a man stared too long, a man

she dreamed of with desire, should she
smile, just a trace, before looking away, or—
oh, did she talk too much? but words

were so numerous, and who knew—
Just then the husband reappeared. The wife
saw the telltale sated glow. *Slut!* she hissed,

contriving her rival's fate: Never again
would she say a word, except to repeat
what was said to her. She would fall

in love with a man who ignored her
altogether, mistaking her echo
for his beloved's strange, half-missing call.


*Face, Mask*

Don't think I sought this affliction.
One day I looked into water,
felt mortality seep into my veins.

That quickly. As if they were dry cloth
seeping wet. The myths claim
the reflection seems like someone else,

but they're wrong. And I'm not
in love. I stare. Even with no wind,
the face won't hold steady. Loss

fills it from behind the way a face
fills a mask. The phenomenon of this
absorbs me. So yes. I'm there

day after day, longing. But if
I could stop, grab a weapon,
go into the woods after deer

I hear behind me, feeding on the real—
I'd miss my shot, to know what it is
to forgive, to be forgiven.


*Weak Claim*

What if I have worn out my days in weeping?
Even if I leaned over water,

my tears disappearing as the surface blurred,
I would not lose sight of you,

my love, whose portrait I carry behind my eyes,
image superimposed

on the world so I can fool myself,
can say, *This is mine*.

*Dream Mouth*

The poet's narcissus, with its magenta-edged corolla,
shimmers in wind, in multiple, a whole
field of them fluttering above the sea

while bones of the dead glow white
as flowers in the shallows where sailing ships
once smashed against rocks in ancient storms.

A man crosses the field, heedless of all but time
and space. Midway, he stops: He has forgotten
something. Something crucial: his name,

his face. He looks for water, finds a small pool.
Ah. He stays there, moving off only at night
to sleep in a bed of flowers, crushing them

with his weight, with the weight of dreams
that open like a pool yielding to a deeper
pool, where he sees his face, beautiful

but mouthless. Not so much freakish
as sad. The sorrow of one who has
understood yet can find no one to tell.

*Arms, Entreaty*

There will be no resolution to this
struggle. The self longs to love
another. But each night, when it
lies down inside its own

arms, it finds itself weeping.
Out of loneliness, yes, and worse.
The body and the world: story
of separation. No matter

what else intervenes—
body, pool, cry—
there is bound to be a
severing, cessation. Otherwise:

No one gathers narcissus into her arms
without thinking death
has been hurried, all for the eye's
insatiable pleasure.


*Coda: Double Jeopardy*

There is no greater loneliness than this:
the image given back, untouchable,
the gaze so fragile even breath disturbs it—
everything desired losing substance.

The image, given back, untouchable,
almost dissolves:
Everything desired, losing substance,
suggesting death,

almost dissolves.
Suddenly, knowledge comes, unstoppable as water,
suggesting death,
not with words but blurred and fleeting cries.

Suddenly, knowledge comes, unstoppable as water:
The gaze, so fragile even breath disturbs it,
not with words but blurred and fleeting cries—
there is no greater loneliness than this.

# FOUR

# De Kooning's Woman

Is she lying asleep in a field
or just hoping to get laid?

Can you really take her for one
of us, or is she too far apart

to be human, her leaf-strewn
haunches miles from her high

round breasts, which seem more
ideas of breasts, dream stuff

you would love to have in hand
and mouth just one more time

to take you back to that original
sweet sin of wanting more than

was your right—more breast
more milk more time more life—

while the trees shake down
leaves into the decaying

world we're forced to abandon—
first breast, then love, then time.

# Elegy, with Towpath and Mule

*after Wolf Kahn's Receding Towpath I*

If I can go along the towpath
looking down at the river

broken into strange geometries
by trees and shrubs,

if I can sense the heavy breath
of mules dragging the barges

forward, the trees
not there, the sun beating down

on the wide vein of the river,
if I can smell the heat

in sweet grass, the gleaming
hide of the mules,

if I can see all this so clearly
I seem to be walking inside

the painting, why is it
hard to imagine you with me,

you who led me from landscape
to landscape, teaching me the names

of all I will some day relinquish
as quietly, I pray, as you did

that summer afternoon
I waited by your bed.

# In a Time of Mourning

After the rain had fallen through her skin
night and day for a month whose name
was washed away, she began to swim
from her body like dreams she had lost

years ago, and nothing impeded her;
she slid through barbed-wire fences,
climbed slick rock faces, kept
going through caves where light

would have seemed a grotesque eruption
from dank wall or floor. She forgot all
the words she'd been stuck in:
*Desire. Betrayal. Ambition.*

Reeds gave way for her; she slipped
over roads like streams. She was being
washed clean. She swam until houses
fell through her hands like water,

until horses and dogs shook wings
and carried her dead to high ground.
It never seemed like prayer. The earth
was mostly water, and she swam.

# The Deepest Blue

### after Wolf Kahn's *The Deepest Blue of Maine*

The deepest blue has ice at its core,
or the idea of ice: It sets your teeth

on edge to look, feeling the rush
of all that cold over your skin,

your body struggling to keep
enough heat to live, let alone swim—

and suppose you had to, suppose
the boat you were in disappeared from

under you the way love sometimes
does—when rage overtakes you,

or your heart goes empty as a room
whose door is loosely hinged—

but we were talking about the deepest
blue, the cold, that sensation in your

veins when you apprehend how short
even the longest life is, the sinking,

the going numb as you drift away
wrapped by blue water, the boat

nowhere to be seen, the horizon
that had seemed such tyranny—

*the end, the end*—no more than
blue deepening into deepest blue.

# Prayer for the Dying

### after Bonnard's *Stairs in the Artist's Garden*

The stairs in the artist's garden
lead to fruit trees and green
where he longs to lie down and sleep

after he has finished painting
the stairs to the garden, the fire
of yellow and orange flowers

on the left, the loose, airy bushes
across the way. I could give the botanical
names for almost everything here,

but I prefer the mystery of effusion—
the dark branches above the last
brick steps like some prehistoric bird

drawn mothlike to the flaming
flowers yet high enough for escape—
singed wings, ash trailing past trees

in the background. Then calm—
enough for centuries—the small birds
quiet with heat, even the crickets

stilled, and the air that made them possible
shimmering just as the stairs curve
toward fruit trees that seem, as the eyes

blur, a yellow house, many windowed,
where the dreamer lives
on bright fruit constantly replenished.

# The Cloud

One morning, though the rhododendrons flutter
in the wind, though the new impatiens open

their white faces, though the lobelia floats
like a deep blue cloud in the center of the garden,

my body feels so heavy I have to drag it
behind me, and after a while of this, trembling

at the effort, I apprehend a rift, as if lightning
had torn the air apart, and suddenly I know

the soul and body are not one, so I stand in joy
of relief that when my body does lie down to die,

there will be this light—the fluttering white face
of memory, blending like a cloud into the night.

# The Gold Basket

### after Sébastien Stoskopff's *Corbeille de verres*

She filled a gold-mesh basket with crystal glasses.
Gently, so none would break.

And none did, until the last one, the one she knew
might be the one-too-many. The shattering

was quick, isolate, less dramatic than her fear
of everything going to pieces. And so what:

It was only a painting. She'd seen it in a museum,
bought a postcard. Still, every night

she lay filling the gold basket with glasses, worried
she was going too far,

and going too far. In this way she became familiar
with grief, which finally requires of us

acceptance but also tact
in the doing: breakage, yes, but not utter ruin.

# Recovery

A narrow road, the rumble of a wide cart,
dust rising in ghosts around the horse neighing,
faintly, under the weight of the household:
blankets and rugs, roped-together utensils.

The man, woman, and child walk behind
toward green, toward water.

Hunger enters the body. It carves a deep cave
near the heart. When night comes,
it makes forays into the dreaming mind:
Low-flying birds appear, even their wings
a succulence. Then day again. More carving.
It strikes against bone. The brain hears a distant ringing.

For answer, hunger carves deeper. The bones
seem a frenzy of sticks in the wind. Birds cry: no:
the body, mouth open, while nothing shoves
its way back and forth among the ribs.

The horse staggers, its bones a frenzy
in the wind. The child holds a stick
like a wand: makes night come with its cape
of glittering holes. Beside her in the cart

her mother and father make the shape of a horse,
of a cloud rearing into a horse, but their grunts

remind her of the pig at the trough,
pig they ate to the last bone,
her mother weeping silently.


They lose count of the days, dreaming toward water.
Then a boat. A long passage. Sickness, groaning,
and in the night the heavy splash of the dead
wrapped and tied and let slide into water.
The child holds her hand in the air like a stick,
like a wand: makes night tear apart into land.
Over and over she does this, and one day it works:
The green is almost blinding. *Eliza*, the man cries,
*Eliza*. The child makes the wand sprinkle life
on her mother's hand, her mother's foot.
Wind brings green from the trees to her lungs.


The child forgets almost everything about this.
She is told stories bearing her name, and she makes them
into a book, many books, whose pages turn
like waves back to water. But whenever she finds a stick
that resembles a wand, she breaks it in two.
She runs through fields that never turn into dust.


One day someone bearing her hands and feet
decides to remember: hunger.

She lets it carve where it will. Empty fields
spread from rib to rib. Dust spills from the backs
of her eyes. There's no way to know dream from waking.

She feels small, light; she travels the surface
of the earth without displacing so much as a stone,
as the dead are said to travel the surface of water.

Her bones ring. She can barely hold one
hand in the other. *Come,* she tells herself.
She walks by fields that fill with green like water.
She walks into years, across earth
that changes even as the night sky
remains the same. She enters the room
where I sit waiting. Hunger so old it feels
ancestral. *Eat,* I tell her. *Live.*

## Continuous Meadow

At the edge of a meadow,
a man carves a figure from a stick.
He gives it curves, powers.

In the trees overhead, loud birds
swoop and thrash, and their shadows
make the man deepen the hollows

of the figure, which is a woman
he has dreamed night after night,
walking toward him from the sea,

her skin glittering so with water
that she looks splattered with stars.
*She must be the night*, he thinks,

and carves her belly into a moon.
He makes her hair the sky's black rush.
Later, drowsed with hunger,

he lies down beside her. She goes on
longer than his breath. He strokes
her arm, leans to listen for her heart.

The world fills with such wonders.

# Then

    after Renoir's *Washhouse at Lower Meudon*


It looks like nothing much, a scene
along a river, skiffs and houseboats,
a boat with sails furled, early morning.

But (the title says) the larger boat's
a washhouse, and maybe those are figures
going in. They could be clothes, draped

over rails and lines to dry. It's all too shimmery
to know, and that's the point: light,
shimmering, and already-the-next-second

while you think about the last, rushing
to keep up as if all life's another language
you're just learning. Of course someone

must have come along—even before
the last brushstroke?—to loosen the ropes
of a skiff, pole off from the bank.

Someone with grief or joy, or maybe just
that watery sense of everything changing
but staying the same. But it's the light

that matters, rushing too fast to comprehend.
How beautiful it is, and must have been,
and will be when you look again.

## Reprise

*after Matisse's Interior with a Violin Case*


Delacroix already painted the violinist:
He's there in the black of the mirror.

The other music comes from birds,
the lyre-backed chair, the cluster of blue
notes where the drapes part. Then the cascade

from clef signatures in the wallpaper,
openings in the balustrade, diagonals
that embrace the horizon (where sea

meets sky). So it could be the interior
of anyone who feels sudden joy

in sweet mortality, the instrument
out of its case, the heart rushing,
the afternoon that will be remembered

for no reason but the moment light
began to pour over the body, all over
the body, like a song it thought forgotten.

## Acknowledgments

Grateful acknowledgment to the editors of the following journals, in which these poems first appeared, sometimes in slightly altered form or under different titles:

| | |
|---|---|
| *American Poetry Journal* | "The Door," "In a Time of Mourning" |
| *Beloit Poetry Journal* | "The Obsessive Gaze" |
| *Blue Fifth Review* (online) | "Bulimia" |
| *Blue Unicorn* | "Continuous Meadow," "Rifts" |
| *Carquinez Poetry Review* | "For All It's Worth," "The Mood of Longing" |
| *convolvulus* | "The Language of Love" |
| *Green Mountains Review* | "Driving Through the Valley," "Wanting" |
| *Marin Poetry Anthology V* | "Love in the Late Afternoon" |
| *National Poetry Review* | "After What Was," "Beyond the Painting" |
| *Natural Bridge* | "Cup" |
| *North Dakota Quarterly* | "Dust" |
| *Northwest Review* | "Early Measures," "A Sentimental Education" |
| *Poetry* | "O, Penelope!" "Prologue" |
| *Poetry Northwest* | "As If Love Were a Room," "The Severing" |
| *RATTLE* | "Against Order" |
| *RUNES* | "Ghost Sailing" |
| *Southern Humanities Review* | "De Kooning's Woman" |
| *Southern Review* | "Resuming Quiet" |

"The Cloud" appeared in *Life as Weather*, which won the Editor's Prize for the 2005 *Two Rivers Review* chapbook competition. "The Deepest Blue" and "Reprise" (as "Despite Elegy") were originally published in *Defying the Flat Surface*, which won the 2005 Ledge Chapbook Award. "Continuous Meadow" won the Rosalie Moore Special Award from *Blue Unicorn* (2002). "Recovery" won the 2006 Lucille Medwick Memorial Award from the Poetry Society of America. "Untimely Snow" appeared in *Deer in Berkeley*, winner of the 2003 *Sow's Ear* Chapbook Award.

About the Author

Lynne Knight's previous collections are *Dissolving Borders* (Quarterly Review of Literature), *The Book of Common Betrayals* (Bear Star Press), and *Night in the Shape of a Mirror* (David Robert Books), plus three award-winning chapbooks. Her cycle of poems on Impressionist winter paintings, *Snow Effects* (Small Poetry Press), has been translated into French by Nicole Courtet. Knight's work has appeared in *Best American Poetry 2000*, and her awards include a Theodore Roethke Award from *Poetry Northwest*, a Lucille Medwick Memorial Award from the Poetry Society of America, and an NEA grant. She lives in Berkeley.

Also from Sixteen Rivers Press:

*Light, Moving*, by Carolyn Miller
*Practice*, by Dan Bellm
*Lucky Break*, by Terry Ehret
*The Opposite of Clairvoyance*, by Gillian Wegener
*Today's Special Dish*, by Nina Lindsay
*In Search of Landscape*, by Helen Wickes
*The Long Night of Flying*, by Sharon Olson
*Any Old Wolf*, by Murray Silverstein
*In the Right Season*, by Diane Sher Lutovich
*Mapmaker of Absences*, by Maria M. Benet
*Swimmer Climbing Onto Shore*, by Gerald Fleming
*No Easy Light*, by Susan Sibbet
*Falling World*, by Lynn Lyman Trombetta
*Sacred Precinct*, by Jacqueline Kudler
*What I Stole*, by Diane Sher Lutovich
*After Cocteau*, by Carolyn Miller
*Snake at the Wrist*, by Margaret Kaufman
*Translations from the Human Language*, by Terry Ehret
*difficult news*, by Valerie Berry

Sixteen Rivers Press is a shared-work, nonprofit poetry collective dedicated to providing an alternative publishing avenue for San Francisco Bay Area poets. Founded in 1999 by seven writers, the press is named for the sixteen rivers that flow into the San Francisco Bay.

SAN JOAQUIN · FRESNO · CHOWCHILLA · MERCED · TUOLUMNE ·
STANISLAUS · CALAVERAS · BEAR · MOKELUMNE · COSUMNES ·
AMERICAN · YUBA · FEATHER · SACRAMENTO · NAPA · PETALUMA